To Patric
from
Kathryn Conroy

THE POEMS OF
ST JOHN OF THE CROSS

These translations are dedicated

TO MARY

THE POEMS OF
ST JOHN OF THE CROSS

The Spanish text
with a translation by

ROY CAMPBELL

Preface by
M. C. D'ARCY, S.J.

Copy 2

PANTHEON BOOKS INC.

Printed in Great Britain for
Pantheon Books, Inc., 333 Sixth Avenue,
New York City

First Edition 1951

The Spanish text of these poems is that of Padre Silverio de Santa Teresa, C.D. ('Obras de San Juan de la Cruz', Burgos, 1929-31), reprinted with his permission. It has previously appeared in England in 'San Juan de la Cruz: Poesías', Liverpool, Institute of Hispanic Studies, 1933, and in 'Poems of St John of the Cross', translated and edited by E. Allison Peers, London, Burns Oates, 1947.

Printed by Hague Gill & Davey Ltd, Pigotts, High Wycombe

Contents

PREFACE

MR ROY CAMPBELL has lived long in Spain and in the years grown in his affection and admiration for the Spanish genius and its faith. It is not surprising, therefore, that as a poet he should translate into English verse one of the great religious poets of Spain. St John of the Cross is an acknowledged master amongst Christian mystics, and a poet in his own right. Just as St Teresa of Avila has won a place in the literature of Spain by the freshness and humanity of her style, so among poets St John, her contemporary and devoted friend, is accepted as supreme in his *genre* by Spanish critics. In the great work of P. Silverio de Santa Teresa, translated and edited by Professor E. Allison Peers, the verdict of Menéndez y Pelayo is quoted. The passage is taken from an address on Mystical Poetry to the Spanish Academy: 'So sublime is this poetry that it scarcely seems to belong to this world at all; it is hardly capable of being assessed by literary criteria. More ardent in its passion than any profane poetry, its form is elegant and exquisite, as plastic and highly figured as any of the finest works of the Renaissance. The Spirit of God has passed through these poems every one, beautifying and sanctifying them on its way.'

For a long time interest in this country was so centred on St Teresa of Avila that St John stood in her shade. The nineteenth century was not seriously attracted to mysticism. Memories of its excesses still lingered: and St Teresa was read more because her character was irresistible than through a desire to follow her mystical way. As is well known, many leading Protestant divines refused to give mysticism a place within the Christian faith, and for a period Catholic spiritual writers advocated a vigorous practice of the virtues in preference to what savoured of illuminism or quietism. In the last fifty years this open or veiled hostility has changed in a marked degree to appreciation. The writings of Evelyn Underhill and Dean Inge stirred the interest of those outside the Catholic Church, while within the Church a host of writers, of whom I need mention only Baron Von Hügel, Abbot Butler, H. Bremond and P. Maréchal, gave a lead to a new and serious study of mystical writings. Among such writings those of St John of the Cross were bound to take a foremost place. They give what many consider the most complete and clear-cut description of the many stages in the mystical ascent.

St John of the Cross was far from any intention to describe his experiences. He was the humblest of men, tiny in body and most retiring of disposition. It was St Teresa who with her genius for reading souls saw through the exterior littleness into the greatness of his spirit, and she singled him out to do for men what she was heroically undertaking in the reform of the nuns of the Carmelite Order. His admiration for and love of St Teresa made him accept what was most repugnant to his nature, and the work he took on his shoulders brought him trials of every kind, many indignities, and even imprisonment by his outraged brethren. Without any preconceived idea of writing, he adopted the habit of jotting down maxims to help others, and at the request of those he thus helped he wrote out for their sake and guidance a treatise for souls entering on the mysterious paths of mystical prayer. Even when doing this he took care, as he thought, only to supplement what he felt St Teresa, with far greater sanctity and experience, was writing. It looks, however, as if the poems just escaped from him; they are stanzas of the spontaneous and semi-ecstatic love song he had always in his heart, once he had come to know God. Many of these poems seem to have been composed when he was imprisoned at Toledo. Others were written at Baeza, a place he loved because in the woods around and by the side of the river Guadalimar he could pass happy hours in union with God. Later, while Prior at Granada, between 1582 and 1585, he wrote the last parts of his prose works as a commentary on the stanzas of the poems.

From this it would appear that poetry was more natural to him than prose: and this is confirmed by the testimony of a nun at the process of his canonisation in 1618.* 'One day he asked this witness in what her prayer consisted, and she replied: "In considering the beauty of God and in rejoicing that He has such beauty". And the Saint was so pleased with this that for some days he said the most sublime things concerning the beauty of God, at which all marvelled. And thus, under the influence of this love, he composed five stanzas, beginning "Beloved let us sing, and in Thy beauty see ourselves portray'd". (*Rejoice, my love, with me*, p. 27). And in all this he showed that there was in his breast a great love of God.' In this artless but vivid account we see how St John was taken out of himself by the simple words of another, and so moved that at the end the ecstasy spilled over into stanzas of love, the Bride crying to the Beloved:

> *Rejoice, my love, with me*
> *And in your beauty see us both reflected:*
> *By mountain-slope and lea*
> *Where purest rills run free*
> *We'll pass into the forest undetected.*

In his versions Mr Roy Campbell has been able to go directly to the Spanish originals, and he is fortunate in that the original Spanish texts have now been edited with care and critical knowledge. For a long time a critical study of these texts was neglected, and readers of St John had to be content with an edition which had been first published in 1703. The well-known English translation by David Lewis, published in 1889, had to be based on this unschol-

*Quoted in *The Complete Works of St John of The Cross*, edited by E. Allison Peers, London, Burns Oates, 1934-5.

[3]

arly text. Fortunately a band of Carmelites in Spain set to work to give us an accurate and authentic text, and they were helped by Fr Benedict Zimmerman and Professor Allison Peers in England. To the latter we owe many important studies on the great Spanish Mystics and also a translation of the truly scientific and recent text in Spanish by P. Silverio de Santa Teresa. Allison Peers in this translation has given us a rendering of the poems in what he himself describes as a 'long and metrically unfettered verse-line'. The great merit of this form of translation is that it serves to let the true likeness of St John appear and avoids the disguise imposed by prose. It also leaves the way open for a poet to try to turn into equivalent English verse what St John has done in Spanish, and moreover to capture the very spirit of the original as Crashaw tried to do with St Teresa.

To do this is a most difficult undertaking. Mystical experience is caviare to the general: it is attained only by the denial of all that we commonly call experience. A new world is discovered which is so different from our familiar one that all our words drawn from our ordinary and familiar experience fail to describe it. They would seem bound in fact to give a wrong impression, as they make us think of what we know instead of this new unknown. In a sense, undoubtedly, mystical experience is ineffable: it would not be that experience if the words used to tell of it were common to it and what we already know. Even within the multiple experience which we all share it is extremely hard to communicate what we may have felt. A man may want to tell us what he felt when he was listening to some music or after meeting someone he loves, or when he met death face to face for the first time; or he may wish to tell us the effect on him of a drug or a spasm of pain or the joy of an unexpected success. The experience is to him unique and all the words he uses could be applicable to something else. It would be easy to argue that private experiences are quite incommunicable; and yet the mysterious fact is that there is a human art of communication which somehow or other overcomes the seemingly insuperable obstacle. The good artist knows that sound and taste, for instance, will help to tell the truth about sight, that we can feel colour and transpose sight into sound. Moreover, by assonances, and associations and by change of rhythm and by heightening the power of words and enlisting our sympathy, he can enable us to relive his own individual experience; and this is precisely what the poet or the great artist does. This is his magic, his gift from God. And this is why neither St John of the Cross nor a translator, like Roy Campbell, refrains from putting into the language of verse what is in itself far more difficult to communicate than the most personal of ordinary human experiences.

To appreciate intelligently the songs of a mystic like St John of the Cross it is essential to grasp the nature of true mysticism. Otherwise such words as

Reveal your presence clearly
And kill me with the beauty you discover,
For pains acquired so dearly
From love, cannot recover
Save only through the presence of the lover.

will in all likelihood be thought to be the description of an intense and very human emotion of the love we know. The truth is that this mystical love cannot even begin until the emotions we are thinking of have been hushed and put to sleep. In our everyday life we are both active and passive, and this is seen very well in our relations with others. They influence our thoughts and behaviour when we are in their presence. A frightened man before an interview can dramatize to himself what he will do and what he will say; but in the interview itself he feels the impact of the other and despite himself may be overpowered by the other's character. Again, our love for the long dead must be very strong for their influence to remain with us and touch us as if they were still alive and present. Now normally we cannot feel any contact with disembodied spirit, and if there be any truth in the supposed communications with the dead, it should be noticed that the contact is on the level of our ordinary sight and by sensible words. In religion, as God is supreme Spirit, our knowledge of Him is indirect, that is to say, by faith or true report. But St John, following the line of the great mystics, in his commentaries on his poems explains how with the grace of God those who are drawn to contemplation may experience the presence of God in a way comparable to that which we enjoy when our friends meet us. The way, however, is exceedingly arduous, so arduous, in fact, as to terrify all except the bravest of lovers. It comes to this, that we must surrender all that is dearest to us in the enjoyment of the senses and go through a dark night in which we live without their help and comfort. Then when this is accomplished we have to sacrifice the prerogative of our own way of thinking and willing and undergo another still darker night in which we have deprived ourselves of all the supports which are familiar to us and make us self-sufficient. This is a kind of death, the making nothing of all that we are to ourselves; but the genuine mystic tells us that when all has been strained away our emptiness will be filled with a new presence; our uncovered soul will receive the contact of divine love, and a new circuit of love will begin, when the soul is passive to an indescribable love which is given to it.

This experience is as remote as can be from the hot life of the senses or even the exalted sharing of human love. Nevertheless just because God is love and man was made in the image of God, the symbolism of human love can be turned to use and made to describe what are the effects of mystical union. How this can be done only a Saint like St John of the Cross can tell us, and he does so by so using language that we know all the time how the images of lover

[6]

and beloved, bridegroom and bride, the *clichés* of love we might almost say, are no more exact than pointer readings; they are copper coins acting as currency for silver. The touch of God is entirely spiritual, and the soul is touched at its source below the level of its activities of thought and will. It is true that the love aroused by this contact may overflow into the emotions and the body and so charge any words used with a supernatural sense, but all the same great artistry and holiness must combine to etherialize the passionate words of sense and make us feel that they have been dipped in some divine spring. There are those who will refuse to believe that this mystical verse is anything more than concealed human passion, and such critics persuade themselves that saints, like St John of the Cross, are victims of some pathological disorder. There is not the slightest evidence for this, so far as I know, in the life of St John, and we have his quiet and strong commentaries on his poems to prove to us what he had in mind when he wrote the poems. To those who have ears to hear, the accents of a genuine experience are unmistakable, and the unprejudiced reader must, I think, become conscious of an unearthly glow in the verse, a strange quality which invades the images and persuades him that there must be a love which is a secret between God and the soul.

In writing this I am assuming that this quality pervades also the translation which Mr Roy Campbell has made of the original Spanish. The reader will be made to realize what the original Spanish is like, how truly a poet St John of the Cross is, and he will, I hope, feel the freshness and the intensity of the mystic and see how the verse leaves the ground and soars to the heights without passing beyond our sight. The ecstatic poems have, too, a movement and metre which belong very closely to the mood, and these have been caught in the translation. The best known of all is the *En Una Noche Oscura*, and we can feel the hush of darkness and the flight of the soul up the secret stair. The Stanzas of the *Spiritual Canticle* are almost equally well known and should be still more appreciated now that the images used stand out in their amazing clarity—that, for instance, of the bridegroom:

> Turn, Ringdove, and alight,
> The wounded stag above
> The slope is now in sight
> Fanned by the wind and freshness of your flight.

In some more measured poems St John combines the theme of love with a statement of some of the Christian mysteries. These make a demand on any translator because extreme accuracy of theological language has to be worked in with the exigencies of the verse. Here we are reminded of the skill of St Thomas Aquinas in composing the *Lauda Sion* and the *Sacris Solemnis*. Lastly there are those poems with refrains, such as, ' And die because I do not die ', and ' Transcending knowledge with my Thought '. Mr Campbell has been most happy, perhaps, in these, because they seem to float so easily into a pattern which some of the greatest English poets have used. Perfect translation hides the sense of translation, and who would guess that such a stanza as the following is not an original?

> This life I live in vital strength
> Is loss of life unless I win You:
> And thus to die I shall continue
> Until I live in You at length.
> Listen (my God!) my life is in You.
> This life I do not want, for I
> Am dying that I do not die.

By rising to this level and maintaining it Mr Roy Campbell carries us with him to Spain and into the presence of a Saint singing of the love of God. He proves, also, as other English poets have proved, that translation can be a stimulus and an original pleasure to a genuine poet.

M. C. D'ARCY, S.J.

[8]

POESÍAS—POEMS

I

Canciones del alma que se goza de haber llega-
do al alto estado de la perección, que es la
unión con Dios, por el camino de la negación
espiritual

En una noche oscura,
Con ansias en amores inflamada,
¡Oh dichosa ventura!
Salí sin ser notada,
Estando ya mi casa sosegada.

A escuras, y segura,
Por la secreta escala disfrazada,
¡Oh dichosa ventura!
A escuras, y en celada,
Estando ya mi casa sosegada.

En la noche dichosa,
En secreto, que nadie me veía,
Ni yo miraba cosa,
Sin otra luz y guía,
Sino la que en el corazón ardía.

Aquesta me guiaba
Más cierto que la luz del mediodía,
A donde me esperaba
Quien yo bien me sabía,
En parte donde nadie parecía.

¡Oh noche, que guiaste,
Oh noche amable más que el alborada:

I

Songs of the soul in rapture at having arrived at the height of perfection, which is union with God by the road of spiritual negation

Upon a gloomy night,
With all my cares to loving ardours flushed,
(O venture of delight!)
With nobody in sight
I went abroad when all my house was hushed.

In safety, in disguise,
In darkness up the secret stair I crept,
(O happy enterprise)
Concealed from other eyes
When all my house at length in silence slept.

Upon that lucky night
In secrecy, inscrutable to sight,
I went without discerning
And with no other light
Except for that which in my heart was burning.

It lit and led me through
More certain than the light of noonday clear
To where One waited near
Whose presence well I knew,
There where no other presence might appear.

Oh night that was my guide!
Oh darkness dearer than the morning's pride,

Oh noche, que juntaste
Amado con amada,
Amada en el Amado transformada!

En mi pecho florido,
Que entero para él sólo se guardaba,
Allí quedó dormido,
Y yo le regalaba,
Y el ventalle de cedros aire daba.

El aire de la almena,
Cuando yo sus cabellos esparcía,
Con su mano serena
En mi cuello hería,
Y todos mis sentidos suspendía.

Quedéme, y olvidéme,
El rostro recliné sobre el Amado,
Cesó todo, y dejéme,
Dejando mi cuidado
Entre las azucenas olvidado.

Oh night that joined the lover
To the beloved bride
Transfiguring them each into the other.

Within my flowering breast
Which only for himself entire I save
He sank into his rest
And all my gifts I gave
Lulled by the airs with which the cedars wave.

Over the ramparts fanned
While the fresh wind was fluttering his tresses,
With his serenest hand
My neck he wounded, and
Suspended every sense with its caresses.

Lost to myself I stayed
My face upon my lover having laid
From all endeavour ceasing:
And all my cares releasing
Threw them amongst the lilies there to fade.

II

Canciones entre el alma y el Esposo

ESPOSA

¿A dónde te escondiste,
Amado, y me dejaste con gemido?
Como el ciervo huiste,
Habiéndome herido;
Salí tras ti clamando, y eras ido.

Pastores, los que fuerdes
Allá por las majadas al otero,
Si por ventura vierdes
Aquel que yo más quiero,
Decidle que adolezco, peno y muero.

Buscando mis amores,
Iré por esos montes y riberas,
Ni cogeré las flores,
Ni temeré las fieras,
Y pasaré los fuertes y fronteras.

PREGUNTA A LAS CRIATURAS

Oh bosques y espesuras,
Plantadas por la mano del Amado,
Oh prado de verduras,
De flores esmaltado,
Decid si por vosotros ha pasado.

RESPUESTA DE LAS CRIATURAS

Mil gracias derramando,
Pasó por estos sotos con presura,
Y yéndolos mirando,
Con sola su figura
Vestidos los dejó de hermosura.

[14]

II

Songs between the soul and the bridegroom

BRIDE
Where can your hiding be,
Beloved, that you left me thus to moan
While like the stag you flee
Leaving the wound with me?
I followed calling loud, but you had flown.

O shepherds, you that, yonder,
Go through the sheepfolds of the slope on high,
If you, as there you wander,
Should chance my love to spy,
Then tell him that I suffer, grieve, and die.

To fetch my loves more near,
Amongst these mountains and ravines I'll stray,
Nor pluck flowers, nor for fear
Of prowling beasts delay,
But pass through forts and frontiers on my way.

QUESTION TO ALL CREATURES
O thickets, densely-trammelled,
Which my love's hand has sown along the height:
O field of green, enamelled
With blossoms, tell me right
If he has passed across you in his flight.

REPLY OF THE CREATURES
Diffusing showers of grace
In haste among these groves his path he took,
And only with his face,
Glancing around the place,
Has clothed them in his beauty with a look.

ESPOSA

¡Ay, quién podrá sanarme!
Acaba de entregarte ya de vero.
No quieras enviarme
De hoy más ya mensajero,
Que no saben decirme lo que quiero.

Y todos cuantos vagan,
De ti me van mil gracias refiriendo
Y todos más me llagan,
Y déjame muriendo
Un no sé qué que quedan balbuciendo.

Mas, ¿cómo perseveras,
Oh vida, no viviendo donde vives,
Y haciendo porque mueras,
Las flechas que recibes,
De lo que del Amado en ti concibes?

¿Por qué, pues has llagado
A aqueste corazón, no le sanaste?
Y pues me le has robado,
¿Por qué así le dejaste,
Y no tomas el robo que robaste?

Apaga mis enojos,
Pues que ninguno basta a deshacellos,
Y véante mis ojos,
Pues eres lumbre dellos,
Y sólo para ti quiero tenellos.

Descubre tu presencia,
Y máteme tu vista y hermosura;
Mira que la dolencia
De amor, que no se cura
Sino con la presencia y la figura.

[16]

BRIDE

Oh who my grief can mend!
Come, make the last surrender that I yearn for,
And let there be an end
Of messengers you send
Who bring me other tidings than I burn for.

All those that haunt the spot
Recount your charm, and wound me worst of all
Babbling I know not what
Strange rapture, they recall,
Which leaves me stretched and dying where I fall.

How can you thus continue
To live, my life, where your own life is not?
With all the arrows in you
And, like a target, shot
By that which in your breast he has begot.

Why then did you so pierce
My heart, nor heal it with your touch sublime?
Why, like a robber fierce,
Desert me every time
And not enjoy the plunder of your crime?

Come, end my sufferings quite
Since no one else suffices for physician:
And let mine eyes have sight
Of you, who are their light,
Except for whom I scorn the gift of vision.

Reveal your presence clearly
And kill me with the beauty you discover,
For pains acquired so dearly
From Love, cannot recover
Save only through the presence of the lover.

¡Oh cristalina fuente,
Si en esos tus semblantes plateados,
Formases de repente
Los ojos deseados,
Que tengo en mis entrañas dibujados!

Apártalos, Amado,
Que voy de vuelo.

ESPOSO

       Vuélvete, paloma,
Que el ciervo vulnerado
Por el otero asoma,
Al aire de tu vuelo, y fresco toma.

ESPOSA

Mi Amado, las montañas,
Los valles solitarios nemorosos,
Las ínsulas extrañas,
Los ríos sonorosos,
El silbo de los aires amorosos.

La noche sosegada
En par de los levantes de la aurora,
La música callada,
La soledad sonora,
La cena, que recrea y enamora.

Nuestro lecho florido,
De cuevas de leones enlazado,
En púrpura tendido,
De paz edificado,
De mil escudos de oro coronado.

O brook of crystal sheen,
Could you but cause, upon your silver fine,
Suddenly to be seen
The eyes for which I pine
Which in my inmost heart my thoughts design!

Withold their gaze, my Love.
For I take wing.

THE BRIDEGROOM
                    Turn, Ringdove, and alight,
The wounded stag above
The slope is now in sight
Fanned by the wind and freshness of your flight.

THE BRIDE
My Love's the mountain range,
The valleys each with solitary grove,
The islands far and strange,
The streams with sounds that change,
The whistling of the lovesick winds that rove.

Before the dawn comes round
Here is the night, dead-hushed with all its glamours,
The music without sound,
The solitude that clamours,
The supper that revives us and enamours.

Now flowers the marriage bed
With dens of lions fortified around it,
With tent of purple spread,
In peace securely founded,
And by a thousand shields of gold surmounted.

[19]

A zaga de tu huella
Las jóvenes discurren al camino
Al toque de centella,
Al adobado vino,
Emisiones de bálsamo Divino.

En la interior bodega
De mi amado bebí, y cuando salía
Por toda aquesta vega,
Ya cosa no sabía,
Y el ganado perdí, que antes seguía.

Allí me dió su pecho,
Allí me enseñó ciencia muy sabrosa,
Y yo le dí de hecho
A mí, sin dejar cosa;
Allí le prometí de ser su esposa.

Mi alma se ha empleado,
Yo todo mi caudal en su servicio:
Ya no guardo ganado,
Ni ya tengo otro oficio;
Que ya sólo en amar es mi ejercicio.

Pues ya si en el ejido
De hoy más no fuere vista ni hallada,
Diréis que me he perdido,
Que andando enamorada,
Me hice perdidiza, y fuí ganada.

De flores y esmeraldas
En las frescas mañanas escogidas,
Haremos las guirnaldas,
En tu amor florecidas,
Y en un cabello mío entretejidas.

Tracking your sandal-mark
The maidens search the roadway for your sign,
Yearning to catch the spark
And taste the scented wine
Which emanates a balm that is divine.

Deep-cellared is the cavern
Of my love's heart, I drank of him alive:
Now, stumbling from the tavern,
No thoughts of mine survive,
And I have lost the flock I used to drive.

He gave his breast; seraphic
In savour was the science that he taught;
And there I made my traffic
Of all, withholding naught,
And promised to become the bride he sought.

My spirit I prepare
To serve him with her riches and her beauty.
No flocks are now my care,
No other toil I share,
And only now in loving is my duty.

So now if from this day
I am not found among the haunts of men,
Say that I went astray
Love-stricken from my way,
That I was lost, but have been found again.

Of flowers and emeralds sheen,
Collected when the dews of dawning shine,
A wreath of garlands green
(That flower for you) we'll twine
Together with one golden hair of mine.

[21]

En solo aquel cabello,
Que en mi cuello volar consideraste,
Mirástele en mi cuello,
Y en él preso quedaste,
Y en uno de mis ojos te llagaste.

Cuando tú me mirabas,
Tu gracia en mí tus ojos imprimían:
Por eso me adamabas,
Y en eso merecían
Los míos adorar lo que en ti vían.

No quieras despreciarme,
Que si color moreno en mí hallaste,
Ya bien puedes mirarme,
Después que me miraste,
Que gracia y hermosura en mí dejaste.

Cogednos las raposas,
Que está ya florecida nuestra viña,
En tanto que de rosas
Hacemos una piña,
Y no parezca nadie en la montiña.

Detente, Cierzo muerto;
Ven, Austro, que recuerdas los amores,
Aspira por mi huerto,
Y corran sus olores,
Y pacerá el Amado entre las flores.

ESPOSO

Entrádose ha la Esposa
En el ameno huerto deseado,
Y a su sabor reposa,
El cuello reclinado
Sobre los dulces brazos del Amado.

[22]

One hair (upon my nape
You loved to watch it flutter, fall, and rise)
Preventing your escape,
Has snared you for a prize
And held you, to be wounded from my eyes.

When you at first surmised me
Your gaze was on my eyes imprinted so,
That it effeminized me,
And my eyes were not slow
To worship that which set your own aglow.

Scorn not my humble ways,
And if my hue is tawny do not loathe me.
On me you well may gaze
Since, after that, the rays
Of every grace and loveliness will clothe me.

Chase all the foxes hence
Because our vine already flowers apace:
And while with roses dense
Our posy we enlace,
Let no one on the hillside show his face.

Cease, then, you arctic gale,
And come, recalling love, wind of the South:
Within my garden-pale
The scent of flowers exhale
Which my Beloved browses with his mouth.

BRIDEGROOM
Now, as she long aspired,
Into the garden comes the bride, a guest:
And in its shade retired
Has leant her neck to rest
Against the gentle arm of the Desired.

[23]

Debajo del manzano,
Allí conmigo fuiste desposada,
Allí te dí la mano,
Y fuiste reparada,
Donde tu madre fuera violada.

A las aves ligeras,
Leones, ciervos, gamos saltadores,
Montes, valles, riberas,
Aguas, aires, ardores,
Y miedos de las noches veladores:

Por las amenas liras
Y canto de serenas os conjuro
Que cesen vuestras iras,
Y no toquéis al muro,
Porque la Esposa duerma más seguro.

ESPOSA

Oh ninfas de Judea,
En tanto que en las flores y rosales
El ámbar perfumea,
Mora en los arrabales,
Y no queráis tocar nuestros umbrales.

Escóndete, Carillo,
Y mira con tu haz a las montañas,
Y no quieras decillo:
Mas mira las compañas
De la que va por ínsulas extrañas.

ESPOSO

La blanca palomica
Al Arca con el ramo se ha tornado,
Y ya la tortolica
Al socio deseado
En las riberas verdes ha hallado.

[24]

Beneath the apple-tree,
You came to swear your troth and to be mated,
Gave there your hand to me,
And have been new-created
There where your mother first was violated.

You birds with airy wings,
Lions, and stags, and roebucks leaping light,
Hills, valleys, creeks, and springs,
Waves, winds, and ardours bright,
And things that rule the watches of the night:

By the sweet lyre and call
Of sirens, now I conjure you to cease
Your tumults one and all,
Nor echo on the wall
That she may sleep securely and at peace.

BRIDE

Oh daughters of Judea,
While yet our flowers and roses in their flesh hold
Ambrosia, come not here,
But keep the outskirts clear,
And do not dare to pass across our threshold.

Look to the mountain peak,
My darling, and stay hidden from the view,
And do not dare to speak
But watch her retinue
Who sails away to islands strange and new.

BRIDEGROOM

The dove so snowy-white,
Returning to the Ark, her frond bestows:
And seeking to unite
The mate of her delight
Has found him where the shady river flows.

[25]

En soledad vivía,
Y en soledad ha puesto ya su nido,
Y en soledad la guía
A solas su querido,
También en soledad de amor herido.

ESPOSA

Gocémonos, Amado,
Y vámonos a ver en tu hermosura
Al monte u al collado,
Do mana el agua pura;
Entremos más adentro en la espesura.

Y luego a las subidas
Cavernas de la piedra nos iremos,
Que están bien escondidas,
Y allí nos entraremos,
Y el mosto de granadas gustaremos.

Allí me mostrarías
Aquello que mi alma pretendía,
Y luego me darías
Allí tú, vida mía,
Aquello que me diste el otro día.

El aspirar del aire,
El canto de la dulce Filomena,
El soto y su donaire,
En la noche serena
Con llama que consume y no da pena.

Que nadie lo miraba,
Aminadab tampoco parecía,
Y el cerco sosegaba,
Y la caballería
A vista de las aguas descendía.

In solitude she bided,
And in the solitude her nest she made:
In solitude he guided
His loved-one through the shade
Whose solitude the wound of love has made.

BRIDE

Rejoice, my love, with me
And in your beauty see us both reflected:
By mountain-slope and lea,
Where purest rills run free,
We'll pass into the forest undetected:

Then climb to lofty places
Among the caves and boulders of the granite,
Where every track effaces,
And, entering, leave no traces,
And revel in the wine of the pomegranate.

Up there, to me you'll show
What my own soul has longed for all the way:
And there, my love, bestow
The secret which you know
And only spoke about the other day.

The breathing air so keen;
The song of Philomel: the waving charm
Of groves in beauty seen:
The evening so serene,
With fire that can consume yet do no harm.

With none our peace offending,
Aminadab has vanished with his slaughters:
And now the siege had ending,
The cavalcades descending
Were seen within the precinct of the waters.

c

III

Canciones del alma en la íntima comunicación
de unión de amor de Dios. Del mismo auctor

¡Oh llama de amor viva,
Que tiernamente hieres
De mi alma en el más profundo centro!
Pues ya no eres esquiva,
Acaba ya si quieres,
Rompe la tela deste dulce encuentro.

¡Oh cauterio suave!
¡Oh regalada llaga!
¡Oh mano blanda! ¡Oh toque delicado,
Que a vida eterna sabe,
Y toda deuda paga!
Matando, muerte en vida la has trocado.

¡Oh lámparas de fuego,
En cuyos resplandores
Las profundas cavernas del sentido,
Que estaba obscuro y ciego,
Con extraños primores
Calor y luz dan junto a su querido!

¡Cuán manso y amoroso
Recuerdas en mi seno,
Donde secretamente solo moras:
Y en tu aspirar sabroso
De bien y gloria lleno
Cuán delicadamente me enamoras!

III

*Song of the soul in intimate communication
and union with the love of God*

Oh flame of love so living,
How tenderly you force
To my soul's inmost core your fiery probe!
Since now you've no misgiving,
End it, pursue your course
And for our sweet encounter tear the robe!

Oh cautery most tender!
Oh gash that is my guerdon!
Oh gentle hand! Oh touch how softly thrilling!
Eternal life you render,
Raise of all debts the burden
And change my death to life, even while killing!

Oh lamps of fiery blaze
To whose refulgent fuel
The deepest caverns of my soul grow bright,
Late blind with gloom and haze,
But in this strange renewal
Giving to the belov'd both heat and light.

What peace, with love enwreathing,
You conjure to my breast
Which only you your dwelling place may call:
While with delicious breathings
In glory, grace, and rest,
So daintily in love you make me fall!

IV

Coplas del mismo hechas sobre un éxtasis de alta contemplación

Entréme donde no supe,
Y quedéme no sabiendo,
Toda sciencia trascendiendo.

Yo no supe dónde entraba,
Pero, cuando allí me ví,
Sin saber dónde me estaba,
Grandes cosas entendí;
No diré lo que sentí,
Que me quedé no sabiendo,
Toda sciencia trascendiendo.

De paz y de piedad
Era la sciencia perfecta,
En profunda soledad,
Entendida vía recta;
Era cosa tan secreta,
Que me quedé balbuciendo,
Toda sciencia trascendiendo.

Estaba tan embebido,
Tan absorto y ajenado,
Que se quedó mi sentido
De todo sentir privado;
Y el espíritu dotado
De un entender no entendiendo,
Toda sciencia trascendiendo.

El que allí llega de vero,
De sí mismo desfallesce;
Cuanto sabía primero

[30]

IV

Verses written after an ecstasy of high exaltation

I entered in, I know not where,
And I remained, though knowing naught,
Transcending knowledge with my thought.

Of when I entered I know naught,
But when I saw that I was there
(Though where it was I did not care)
Strange things I learned, with greatness fraught.
Yet what I heard I'll not declare.
But there I stayed, though knowing naught,
Transcending knowledge with my thought.

Of peace and piety interwound
This perfect science had been wrought,
Within the solitude profound
A straight and narrow path it taught,
Such secret wisdom there I found
That there I stammered, saying naught,
But topped all knowledge with my thought.

So borne aloft, so drunken-reeling,
So rapt was I, so swept away,
Within the scope of sense or feeling
My sense or feeling could not stay.
And in my soul I felt, revealing,
A sense that, though its sense was naught,
Transcended knowledge with my thought.

The man who truly there has come
Of his own self must shed the guise;
Of all he knew before the sum

Mucho bajo le paresce;
Y su sciencia tanto cresce,
Que se queda no sabiendo,
Toda sciencia trascendiendo.

Cuanto más alto se sube,
Tanto menos entendía
Qué es la tenebrosa nube
Que a la noche esclarecía;
Por eso quien la sabía
Queda siempre no sabiendo
Toda sciencia trascendiendo.

Este saber no sabiendo
Es de tan alto poder,
Que los sabios arguyendo
Jamás le pueden vencer;
Que no llega su saber
A no entender entendiendo,
Toda sciencia trascendiendo.

Y es de tan alta excelencia
Aqueste sumo saber,
Que no hay facultad ni sciencia
Que le puedan emprender;
Quien se supiere vencer
Con un no saber sabiendo,
Irá siempre trascendiendo.

Y si lo queréis oír,
Consiste esta suma sciencia
En un subido sentir
De la divinal Esencia;
Es obra de su clemencia
Hacer quedar no entendiendo
Toda sciencia trascendiendo.

Seems far beneath that wondrous prize:
And in this lore he grows so wise
That he remains, though knowing naught,
Transcending knowledge with his thought.

The farther that I climbed the height
The less I seemed to understand
The cloud so tenebrous and grand
That there illuminates the night.
For he who understands that sight
Remains for aye, though knowing naught,
Transcending knowledge with his thought.

This wisdom without understanding
Is of so absolute a force
No wise man of whatever standing
Can ever stand against its course,
Unless they tap its wondrous source,
To know so much, though knowing naught,
They pass all knowledge with their thought.

This summit all so steeply towers
And is of excellence so high
No human faculties or powers
Can ever to the top come nigh.
Whoever with its steep could vie,
Though knowing nothing, would transcend
All thought, forever, without end.

If you would ask, what is its essence—
This summit of all sense and knowing:
It comes from the Divinest Presence—
The sudden sense of Him outflowing,
In His great clemency bestowing
The gift that leaves men knowing naught,
Yet passing knowledge with their thought.

V

Coplas del alma que pena por ver a Dios, del mismo auctor

Vivo sin vivir en mí,
Y de tal manera espero,
Que muero porque no muero.

En mí yo no vivo ya,
Y sin Dios vivir no puedo;
Pues sin él y sin mí quedo,
Este vivir ¿qué será?
Mil muertes se me hará,
Pues mi misma vida espero,
Muriendo porque no muero.

Esta vida que yo vivo
Es privación de vivir;
Y así, es contino morir
Hasta que viva contigo.
Oye, mi Dios, lo que digo,
Que esta vida no la quiero;
Que muero porque no muero.

Estando absente de ti,
¿Qué vida puedo tener,
Sino muerte padescer,
La mayor que nunca vi?
Lástima tengo de mí,
Pues de suerte persevero,
Que muero porque no muero.

El pez que del agua sale,
Aun de alivio no caresce,

V

Coplas about the soul which suffers with impatience to see God

I live without inhabiting
Myself—in such a wise that I
Am dying that I do not die.

Within myself I do not dwell
Since without God I cannot live.
Reft of myself, and God as well,
What serves this life (I cannot tell)
Except a thousand deaths to give?
Since waiting here for life I lie
And die because I do not die.

This life I live in vital strength
Is loss of life unless I win You:
And thus to die I shall continue
Until in You I live at length.
Listen (my God!) my life is in You.
This life I do not want, for I
Am dying that I do not die.

Thus in your absence and your lack
How can I in myself abide
Nor suffer here a death more black
Than ever was by mortal died.
For pity of myself I've cried
Because in such a plight I lie
Dying because I do not die.

The fish that from the stream is lost
Derives some sort of consolation

Que en la muerte que padesce,
Al fin la muerte le vale.
¿Qué muerte habrá que se iguale
A mi vivir lastimero,
Pues si más vivo más muero?

Cuando me pienso aliviar
De verte en el Sacramento,
Háceme más sentimiento
El no te poder gozar;
Todo es para más penar,
Por no verte como quiero,
Y muero porque no muero.

Y si me gozo, Señor,
Con esperanza de verte,
En ver que puedo perderte
Se me dobla mi dolor:
Viviendo en tanto pavor,
Y esperando como espero,
Muérome porque no muero.

Sácame de aquesta muerte,
Mi Dios, y dame la vida;
No me tengas impedida
En este lazo tan fuerte;
Mira que peno por verte,
Y mi mal es tan entero,
Que muero porque no muero.

Lloraré mi muerte ya,
Y lamentaré mi vida
En tanto que detenida
Por mis pecados está.
¡Oh mi Dios! ¿cuándo será?
Cuando yo diga de vero:
Vivo ya porque no muero.

That in his death he pays the cost
At least of death's annihilation.
To this dread life with which I'm crossed
What fell death can compare, since I,
The more I live, the more must die.

When thinking to relieve my pain
I in the sacraments behold You
It brings me greater grief again
That to myself I cannot fold You.
And that I cannot see you plain
Augments my sorrow, so that I
Am dying that I do not die.

If in the hope I should delight,
Oh Lord, of seeing You appear,
The thought that I might lose Your sight,
Doubles my sorrow and my fear.
Living as I do in such fright,
And yearning as I yearn, poor I
Must die because I do not die.

Oh rescue me from such a death
My God, and give me life, not fear;
Nor keep me bound and struggling here
Within the bonds of living breath.
Look how I long to see You near,
And how in such a plight I lie
Dying because I do not die!

I shall lament my death betimes,
And mourn my life, that it must be
Kept prisoner by sins and crimes
So long before I am set free:
Ah God, my God, when shall it be?
When I may say (and tell no lie)
I live because I've ceased to die?

[37]

VI

Otras del mismo a lo divino

Tras de un amoroso lance,
Y no de esperanza falto,
Volé tan alto, tan alto,
Que le dí a la caza alcance.

Para que yo alcance diese
A aqueste lance divino,
Tanto volar me convino,
Que de vista me perdiese;
Y con todo, en este trance
En el vuelo quedé falto;
Mas el amor fué tan alto,
Que le dí a la caza alcance.

Cuando más alto subía,
Deslumbróseme la vista,
Y la más fuerte conquista
En escuro se hacía;
Mas por ser de amor el lance
Dí un ciego y oscuro salto,
Y fuí tan alto, tan alto,
Que le dí a la caza alcance.

Cuanto más alto llegaba
De este lance tan subido,
Tanto más bajo y rendido
Y abatido me hallaba.
Dije: No habrá quien alcance;
Y abatíme tanto, tanto,
Que fuí tan alto, tan alto.
Que le dí a la caza alcance.

[38]

VI

*Other verses with a divine meaning
by the same author*

Not without hope did I ascend
Upon an amorous quest to fly
And up I soared so high, so high,
I seized my quarry in the end.

As on this falcon quest I flew
To chase a quarry so divine,
I had to soar so high and fine
That soon I lost myself from view.
With loss of strength my plight was sorry
From straining on so steep a course.
But love sustained me with such force
That in the end I seized my quarry.

The more I rose into the height
More dazzled, blind, and lost I spun.
The greatest conquest ever won
I won in blindness, like the night.
Because love urged me on my way
I gave that mad, blind, reckless leap
That soared me up so high and steep
That in the end I seized my prey.

The steeper upward that I flew
On so vertiginous a quest
The humbler and more lowly grew
My spirit, fainting in my breast.
I said ' None yet can find the way '
But as my spirit bowed more low,
Higher and higher did I go
Till in the end I seized my prey.

[39]

Por una extraña manera
Mil vuelos pasé de un vuelo,
Porque esperanza de cielo
Tanto alcanza cuanto espera;
Esperé sólo este lance,
Y en esperar no fuí falto,
Pues fuí tan alto, tan alto,
Que le dí a la caza alcance.

By such strange means did I sustain
A thousand starry flights in one,
Since hope of Heaven yet by none
Was ever truly hoped in vain.
Only by hope I won my way
Nor did my hope my aim belie,
Since I soared up so high, so high,
That in the end I seized my prey.

VII

Otras canciones a lo divino (del mismo autor) de Cristo y el alma

Un pastorcico solo está penado,
Ajeno de placer y de contento,
Y en su pastora puesto el pensamiento,
Y el pecho del amor muy lastimado.

No llora por haberle amor llagado,
Que no le pena verse así afligido,
Aunque en el corazón está herido;
Mas llora por pensar que está olvidado.

Que sólo de pensar que está olvidado
De su bella pastora, con gran pena
Se deja, maltratar en tierra ajena,
El pecho del amor muy lastimado.

Y dice el Pastorcico: ¡Ay, desdichado
De aquel que de mi amor ha hecho ausencia,
Y no quiere gozar la mi presencia,
Y el pecho por su amor muy lastimado!

Y a cabo de un gran rato se ha encumbrado
Sobre un árbol do abrió sus brazos bellos,
Y muerto se ha quedado, asido de ellos,
El pecho del amor muy lastimado.

VII

Other songs concerning Christ and the soul

A shepherd lad was mourning his distress,
Far from all comfort, friendless and forlorn.
He fixed his thought upon his shepherdess
Because his breast by love was sorely torn.

He did not weep that love had pierced him so,
Nor with self-pity that the shaft was shot,
Though deep into his heart had sunk the blow,
It grieved him more that he had been forgot.

Only to think that he had been forgotten
By his sweet shepherdess, with travail sore,
He let his foes (in foreign lands begotten)
Gash the poor breast that love had gashed before.

'Alas! Alas! for him', the Shepherd cries,
'Who tries from me my dearest love to part
So that she does not gaze into my eyes
Or see that I am wounded to the heart.'

Then, after a long time, a tree he scaled,
Opened his strong arms bravely wide apart,
And clung upon that tree till death prevailed,
So sorely was he wounded in his heart.

VIII

Cantar del alma que se huelga de conoscer
a Dios por fe

Que bien sé yo la fonte que mana y corre,
Aunque es de noche.

Aquella eterna fonte está ascondida,
Que bien sé yo do tiene su manida,
Aunque es de noche.

Su origen no lo sé, pues no le tiene,
Mas sé que todo origen de ella viene,
Aunque es de noche.

Sé que no puede ser cosa tan bella,
Y que cielos y tierra beben de ella,
Aunque es de noche.

Bien sé que suelo en ella no se halla,
Y que ninguno puede vadealla,
Aunque es de noche.

Su claridad nunca es escurecida,
Y sé que toda luz de ella es venida,
Aunque es de noche.

Sé ser tan caudalosas sus corrientes,
Que infiernos, cielos riegan, y las gentes,
Aunque es de noche.

El corriente que nace de esta fuente,
Bien sé que es tan capaz y omnipotente,
Aunque es de noche.

[44]

VIII

Song of the soul that is glad to know God by faith

How well I know that fountain's rushing flow
Although by night

Its deathless spring is hidden. Even so
Full well I guess from whence its sources flow
Though it be night.

Its origin (since it has none) none knows:
But that all origin from it arose
Although by night.

I know there is no other thing so fair
And earth and heaven drink refreshment there
Although by night.

Full well I know its depth no man can sound
And that no ford to cross it can be found
Though it be night

Its clarity unclouded still shall be:
Out of it comes the light by which we see
Though it be night.

Flush with its banks the stream so proudly swells;
I know it waters nations, heavens, and hells
Though it be night.

The current that is nourished by this source
I know to be omnipotent in force
Although by night.

El corriente que de estas dos procede
Sé que ninguna de ellas le precede,
Aunque es de noche.

Aquesta eterna fonte está escondida
En este vivo pan por darnos vida,
Aunque es de noche.

Aquí se está llamando a las criaturas,
Y de esta agua se hartan, aunque a escuras,
Porque es de noche.

Aquesta viva fuente, que deseo,
En este pan de vida yo la veo,
Aunque de noche.

From source and current a new current swells
Which neither of the other twain excels
Though it be night.

The eternal source hides in the Living Bread
That we with life eternal may be fed
Though it be night.

Here to all creatures it is crying, hark!
That they should drink their fill though in the dark,
For it is night.

This living fount which is to me so dear
Within the bread of life I see it clear
Though it be night.

IX

ROMANCE I

Sobre el Evangelio 'In principio erat Verbum'
acerca de la Santísima Trinidad

En el principio moraba
El Verbo, y en Dios vivía,
En quien su felicidad
Infinita poseía.

El mismo Verbo Dios era,
Que el principio se decía;
Él moraba en el principio,
Y principio no tenía.

Él era el mismo principio;
Por eso de él carecía;
El Verbo se llama Hijo
Que del principio nacía.

Hale siempre concebido,
Y siempre le concebía,
Dale siempre su sustancia,
Y siempre se la tenía.

Y así, la gloria del Hijo
Es la que en el Padre había,
Y toda su gloria el Padre
En el Hijo poseía.

Como amado en el amante
Uno en otro residía,
Y aquese amor que los une,
En lo mismo convenía.

IX

*Upon the Gospel 'In the Beginning was the
Word' relating to the Most Holy Trinity*

In the beginning of all things
The Word lived in the Lord at rest.
And His felicity in Him
Was from infinity possessed.

That very Word was God Himself
By which all being was begun
For He lived in the beginning
And beginning had He none.

He Himself was the beginning,
So He had none, being one.
What was born of the beginning
Was the Word we call the Son.

Even so has God conceived Him
And conceived Him always so,
Ever giving Him the substance
As He gave it long ago.

And thus the glory of the Son
Is the glory of the Sire
And the glory of the Father
From His Son He does acquire.

As the loved-one in the lover
Each in the other's heart resided:
And the love that makes them one
Into one of them divided,

Con el uno y con el otro
En igualdad y valía:
Tres Personas y un amado
Entre todos tres había.

Y un amor en todas ellas
Y un amante las hacía;
Y el amante es el amado
En que cada cual vivía;

Que el ser que los tres poseen,
Cada cual le poseía,
Y cada cual de ellos ama
A la que este ser tenía.

Este ser es cada una,
Y éste sólo las unía
En un inefable nudo
Que decir no se sabía.

Por lo cual era infinito
El amor que las unía,
Porque un solo amor tres tienen,
Que su esencia se decía;
Que el amor, cuanto más uno,
Tanto más amor hacía.

Then with one and with the other
Mated in such equality,
Three Persons now and one Beloved
They numbered, though they still were three.

There is one love in all three Persons:
One lover all the Three provides;
And the beloved is the lover
Which in each of them resides.

The Being which all three possess
Each of them does possess alone:
And each of them loves what that Being
Itself possesses of its own.

This very Being is Each One,
And it alone, in its own way,
Has bound them in that wondrous knot
Whose mystery no man can say.

Thus lives undying and eternal
The love that has entwined them so,
Because one love the three united
Which as their Essence now we know,
And this one love, the more in one-ness,
The more and more in love will grow.

X

ROMANCE II

De la comunicación de las tres Personas

En aquel amor inmenso
Que de los dos procedía,
Palabras de gran regalo
El Padre al Hijo decía,

De tan profundo deleite,
Que nadie las entendía;
Sólo el Hijo lo gozaba,
Que es a quien pertenecía.

Pero aquello que se entiende
De esta manera decía:
Nada me contenta, Hijo,
Fuera de tu compañía.

Y si algo me contenta,
En ti mismo lo quería;
El que a ti más se parece,
A mí más satisfacía.

Y el que nada te semeja,
En mí nada hallaría;
En ti sólo me he agradado,
¡Oh vida de vida mía!

X

ROMANCE II

Of the communion of the three Persons

Out of the love immense and bright
That from the two had thus begun,
Words of ineffable delight
The Father spoke unto the Son:

Words of so infinite a rapture
Their drift by none could be explained:
Only the Son their sense could capture
That only to Himself pertained.

What of them we can sense the clearest
Was in this manner said and thought:
Out of Your company, my Dearest,
I can be satisfied by nought.

But if aught please me, I as duly
In You, Yourself, the cause construe.
The one who satisfies Me truly
Is him who most resembles You.

He who in naught resembles You
Shall find of Me no trace or sign,
Life of My Life! for only through
Your own can I rejoice in Mine.

Eres lumbre de mi lumbre,
Eres mi sabiduría,
Figura de mi sustancia,
En quien bien me complacía.

Al que a ti te amare, Hijo,
A mí mismo le daría,
Y el amor yo en ti tengo,
Ese mismo en él pondría,
En razón de haber amado
A quien yo tanto quería.

You are the brilliance of My light
My wisdom and My power divine,
The figure of My substance bright
In whom I am well pleased to shine!

The man who loves You, O my Son,
To him Myself I will belong.
The love that in Yourself I won
I'll plant in him and root it strong,
Because he loved the very one
I loved so deeply and so long.

XI

ROMANCE III

De la Creación

Una esposa que te ame,
Mi Hijo, darte quería,
Que por tu valor merezca
Tener nuestra compañía.

Y comer pan a una mesa,
Del mismo que yo comía;
Porque conozca los bienes
Que en tal Hijo yo tenía.
Y se congracie conmigo
De tu gracia y lozanía.

Mucho lo agradezco, Padre,
El Hijo le respondía;
A la esposa que me dieres,
Yo mi claridad daría,

Para que por ella vea
Cuánto mi Padre valía,
Y cómo el ser que poseo,
De su ser le recibía.

Reclinarla he yo en mi brazo
Y en tu amor se abrasaría,
Y con eterno deleite
Tu bondad sublimaría.

XI

ROMANCE III

Of the Creation

I wish to give You, My dear Son,
To cherish You, a lovely bride,
And one who for Your worth will merit
To live forever by Our side.

And she will eat bread at our table
The selfsame bread on which I've fed:
That she may know the worth and value
Of the Son whom I have bred,
And there enjoy with Me forever
The grace and glory that You shed.

'Thanks to You, Almighty Father,'
The Son made answer to the Sire,
'To the wife that You shall give Me
I shall give My lustrous fire,

'That by its brightness she may witness
How infinite My Father's worth
And how My being from Your being
In every way derived its birth.

'I'll hold her on My arm reclining
And with Your love will burn her so
That with an endless joy and wonder
Your loving kindness she may know.'

XII

ROMANCE IV

Hágase, pues, dijo el Padre,
Que tu amor lo merecía:
Y en este dicho que dijo,
El mundo criado había.

Palacio para la esposa,
Hecho en gran sabiduría;
El cual, en dos aposentos,
Alto y bajo, dividía.

El bajo de diferencias
Infinitas componía;
Mas el alto hermoseaba
De admirable pedrería.

Porque conozca la esposa
El Esposo que tenía,
En el alto colocaba
La angélica jerarquía;

Pero la natura humana
En el bajo la ponía,
Por ser en su compostura
Algo de menor valía.

Y aunque el ser y los lugares
De esta suerte los partía,
Pero todos son un cuerpo
De la esposa que decía:

XII

ROMANCE IV

'Let it be done, then,' said the Father,
'For Your love's surpassing worth.'
And the moment he pronounced it
Was the creation of the Earth.

For the bride He built a palace
Out of His knowledge vast and grand,
Which in two separate compartments,
One high, one low, He wisely planned.

The lower storey was of endless
Differences composed: the higher
He beautified with wondrous jewels,
Refulgent with supernal fire.

That the bride might know her Bridegroom
In the true glory of His power,
In the top part He set the angels
In shining hierarchy to tower.

But, tenant of the lower mansion
Our human nature was assigned
Because its human composition
Falls short of the angelic kind.

And though the Being in two places
He divided in this way,
He composed of both one body
To house the Bride, who thus did say:

Que el amor de un mismo Esposo
Una Esposa los hacía:
Los de arriba poseían
El Esposo en alegría;

Los de abajo en esperanza
De fe que les infundía,
Diciéndoles que algún tiempo
Él los engrandecería.

Y que aquella su bajeza
Él se la levantaría,
De manera que ninguno
Ya la vituperaría.

Porque en todo semejante
Él a ellos se haría,
Y se vendría con ellos,
Y con ellos moraría.

Y que Dios sería hombre,
Y que el hombre Dios sería,
Y trataría con ellos,
Comería y bebería.

Y que con ellos continuo
Él mismo se quedaría,
Hasta que se consumase
Este siglo que corría.

Cuando se gozaran juntos
En eterna melodía;
Porque él era la cabeza
De la esposa que tenía.

[60]

That the love of one sole Bridegroom
Made them into one sole Bride.
Those of the upper part possessed Him
In deathless joy beatified:

Those underneath, in hope and yearning,
Born of the faith He brings to birth,
By telling them that surely, sometime,
His love will magnify their worth;

And all in them that's base and lowly
He would exalt to such degree
That none who after that beheld it
Would scorn its first humility.

Exactly, in all things like they are,
He would cause Himself to be.
He would traffic in their dealings
And in their daily life agree.

And so the God would be the Man
And the Man be the God: and then
He would roam amongst them freely
And eat and drink with other men.

He will stay with us forever.
As a Comrade He will stay,
Till the present dispensation
Is consumed and fades away.

Then, to a deathless music sounding,
Bride to Bridegroom will be pressed,
Because He is the crown and headpiece
Of the Bride that He possessed.

A la cual todos los miembros
De los justos juntaría,
Que son cuerpo de la esposa,
A la cual él tomaría.

En sus brazos tiernamente,
Y allí su amor la daría;
Y que así juntos en uno
Al Padre la llevaría.

Donde del mismo deleite
Que Dios goza, gozaría;
Que, como el Padre y el Hijo,
Y el que de ellos procedía,

El uno vive en el otro;
Así la esposa sería,
Que, dentro de Dios absorta,
Vida de Dios viviría.

To her beauty all the members
Of the just He will enlace
To form the body of the Bride
When taken into His embrace.

Tenderly in His arms He'll take her
With all the force that God can give
And draw her nearer to the Father
All in one unison to live.

There with the single, same rejoicing
With which God revels, she will thrill,
Revelling with the Son, the Father,
And that which issues from Their will,

Each one living in the other;
Samely loved, clothed, fed, and shod.
She, absorbed in Him forever,
She will live the Life of God.

XIII

ROMANCE V

Con esta buena esperanza
Que de arriba les venía,
El tedio de sus trabajos
Más leve se les hacía;

Pero la esperanza larga
Y el deseo que crecía
De gozarse con su Esposo
Continuo les afligía.

Por lo cual con oraciones,
Con suspiros y agonía,
Con lágrimas y gemidos
Le rogaban noche y día

Que ya se determinase
A les dar su compañía.
Unos decían: ¡Oh, si fuese
En mi tiempo el alegría!

Otros: Acaba, Señor;
Al que has de enviar envía.
Otros: Oh si ya rompieses
Esos cielos, y vería

Con mis ojos, que bajases,
Y mi llanto cesaría;
Regad, nubes de lo alto,
Que la tierra lo pedía,

Y ábrase ya la tierra,
Que espinas nos producía,
Y produzca aquella flor
Con que ella florecería.

XIII

ROMANCE V

With the blest hope of this union
Coming to them from on high,
All the tedium of their labour
Seemed to glide more lightly by.

But the length of endless waiting
And the increase of desire
To enjoy the blessed Bridegroom
Was to them affliction dire.

So they made continual prayer
With sighs of piteous dismay,
And with groans and lamentations
Pleaded with Him night and day

That He would decide with them
To share His company at last.
'Oh if but this thing could happen',
They cried, 'before our time be past.'

Others cried: 'Come Lord and end it!
Him You have promised, send Him now!'
Others: 'If only You would sunder
Those skies, and to my sight allow

'The vision of Yourself descending
To make my lamentations cease;
Cloud in the height, rain down upon us
That the earth may find release.

'Let the earth be cleft wide open
That bore us thorns so sharp and sour
And now at last produce the Blossom
With which it was ordained to flower.'

Otros decían: ¡Oh dichoso
El que en tal tiempo sería,
Que merezca ver a Dios
Con los ojos que tenía,

Y tratarle con sus manos,
Y andar en su compañía,
Y gozar de los misterios
Que entonces ordenaría!

Others said: 'Oh happy people
Who will be living in those years
And will deserve to see the Bridegroom
With their own eyes when He appears:

'Who with their own hands then will touch Him,
And walk in friendship by His side,
And there enjoy the sacred mysteries,
That in His reign He will provide.'

XIV

ROMANCE VI

En aquestos y otros ruegos
Gran tiempo pasado había;
Pero en los postreros años
El fervor mucho crecía.

Cuando el viejo Simeón
En deseo se encendía,
Rogando a Dios que quisiese
Dejalle ver este día.

Y así, el Espíritu Santo
Al buen viejo respondía
Que le daba su palabra
Que la muerte no vería

Hasta que la vida viese,
Que de arriba decendía,
Y que él en sus mismas manos
Al mismo Dios tomaría,
Y le tendría en sus brazos,
Y consigo abrazaría.

XIV

ROMANCE VI

In these and other supplications
A long age went slowly past,
But in later times the longing
Grew so fervent that, at last,

The aged Simeon, taking fire
With inward love, knelt down to pray,
Beseeching God that He would grant him
He might be spared to see the day.

And the Holy Spirit answering
To his pleadings made reply
Giving him His word that truly
He would never come to die

Till from on high he should behold
The Light descending on its quest,
Till he took in his own hands
God Himself, to be caressed,
Folded his arms about Him fondly
And held Him closely to his breast.

XV

ROMANCE VII

Prosigue la Encarnación

Ya que el tiempo era llegado
En que hacerse convenía
El rescate de la esposa
Que en duro yugo servía,

Debajo de aquella ley
Que Moisés dado le había,
El Padre con amor tierno
De esta manera decía:

Ya ves, Hijo, que a tu esposa
A tu imagen hecho había,
Y en lo que a ti se parece
Contigo bien convenía;

Pero difiere en la carne,
Que en tu simple ser no había;
En los amores perfectos
Esta ley se requería,

Que se haga semejante
El amante a quien quería,
Que la mayor semejanza
Más deleite contenía.

El cual sin duda en tu esposa
Grandemente crecería
Si te viere semejante
En la carne que tenía.

[70]

XV

ROMANCE VII

Continues the Incarnation

Now that the time was truly come
The ancient order to revoke
And pay the ransom of the bride
Serving in so hard a yoke,

Under that former law which Moses
Of old upon her shoulders laid—
The Father, in His love most tender,
To the Son, His thought displayed:

'You see how Your beloved bride
After Your image has been made.
In what she most resembles You
Her loveliness I have arrayed,

'Though differing from You by that flesh
Your finer nature never knew;
There is in every perfect love
A law to be accomplished too:

'That the lover should resemble
The belov'd: and be the same.
And the greater is the likeness
Brighter will the rapture flame.

'That which to Your own beloved
Greater rapture would provide
Would be to behold that likeness
In the flesh with her allied.'

Mi voluntad es la tuya,
El Hijo le respondía,
Y la gloria que yo tengo,
Es tu voluntad ser mía.

Y a mí me conviene, Padre,
Lo que tu Alteza decía,
Porque por esta manera
Tu bondad más se vería.

Veráse tu gran potencia,
Justicia y sabiduría,
Irélo a decir al mundo,
Y noticia le daría
De tu belleza y dulzura
Y de tu soberanía.

Iré a buscar a mi esposa,
Y sobre mí tomaría
Sus fatigas y trabajos,
En que tanto padescía.

Y porque ella vida tenga,
Y por ella moriría,
Y sacándola del lago,
A ti te la volvería.

The Son then answered to the Father,
'My will is Yours and Yours alone,
And the glory that I shine with
Is My will to work Your own.

'That which Your Grace says, O My Father,
In everything appears the best
Since most clearly in this manner
Can Your kindness be professed.

'Thus Your omnipotence, and justice,
And wisdom will be well descried,
I will tell it to the world,
And spread the tidings far and wide
Of Your beauty, power, and sweetness
In one sovereignty allied.'

'I will go now and seek My bride,
And take upon My shoulders strong
The cares, the weariness, and labours
Which she has suffered for so long.

And that she may win new life
I myself for her will die,
Rescue her from the burning lake,
And bear her back to You on high.'

XVI

ROMANCE VIII

Prosigue

Entonces llamó un arcángel,
Que San Gabriel se decía,
Y envióle a una doncella
Que se llamaba María,

De cuyo consentimiento
El misterio se hacía;
En la cual la Trinidad
De carne al Verbo vestía.

Y aunque tres hacen la obra,
En el uno se hacía;
Y quedó el Verbo encarnado
En el vientre de María.

Y el que tenía sólo Padre,
Ya también Madre tenía,
Aunque no como cualquiera
Que de varón concebía;

Que de las entrañas de ella
Él su carne recibía:
Por lo cual Hijo de Dios
Y del hombre se decía.

XVI

ROMANCE VIII

The same

Then He summoned an archangel,
Saint Gabriel: and when he came,
Sent him forth to find a maiden,
      Mary was her name.

Only through her consenting love
Could the mystery be preferred
That the Trinity in human
      Flesh might clothe the Word.

Though the three Persons worked the wonder
It only happened in the One.
So was the Word made incarnation
      In Mary's womb, a son.

So He who only had a Father
Now had a Mother undefiled,
Though not as ordinary maids
      Had she conceived the Child.

By Mary, and with her own flesh
He was clothed in His own frame:
Both Son of God and Son of Man
      Together had one name.

XVII

ROMANCE IX

Del Nacimiento

Ya que era llegado el tiempo
En que de nacer había,
Así como desposado
De su tálamo salía,

Abrazado con su esposa,
Que en sus brazos la traía,
Al cual la graciosa Madre
En un pesebre ponía,

Entre unos animales
Que a la sazón allí había:
Los hombres decían cantares,
Los ángeles melodía,

Festejando el desposorio
Que entre tales dos había;
Pero Dios en el pesebre
Allí lloraba y gemía,

Que eran joyas que la esposa
Al desposorio traía;
Y la Madre estaba en pasmo
De que tal trueque veía;

El llanto del hombre en Dios,
Y en el hombre la alegría,
Lo cual del uno y del otro
Tan ajeno ser solía.

XVII

ROMANCE IX

The Birth of Christ

Now that the season was approaching
Of His long-expected birth,
Like a bridegroom from his chamber
He emerged upon our earth

Clinging close to His beloved
Whom He brought along with Him.
While the gracious Mary placed them
In a manger damp and dim.

Amongst the animals that round it
At that season stretched their limbs,
Men were singing songs of gladness
And the angels chanting hymns,

To celebrate the wondrous marriage
By whose bond such two were tied,
But the wee God in the manger
He alone made moan and cried;

Tears were the jewels of the dowry
Which the bride with her had brought.
And the Mother gazed upon them
Nearly fainting at the thought.

The tears of Man in God alone,
The joy of God in men was seen.
Two things so alien to each other,
Or to the rule, had never been.

[77]

XVIII

Otro del mismo que va por 'Super flumina Babylonis'

Encima de las corrientes,
Que en Babilonia hallaba,
Allí me senté llorando,
Allí la tierra regaba.

Acordándome de ti,
Oh Sión, a quien amaba,
Era dulce tu memoria,
Y con ella más lloraba.

Dejé los trajes de fiesta,
Los de trabajo tomaba,
Y colgué en los verdes sauces
La música que llevaba.

Poniéndola en esperanza
De aquello que en ti esperaba;
Allí me hirió el amor,
Y el corazón me sacaba.

Díjele que me matase,
Pues de tal suerte llagaba:
Yo me metía en su fuego,
Sabiendo que me abrasaba,

Desculpando el avecica
Que en el fuego se acababa;
Estábame en mí muriendo,
Y en ti sólo respiraba.

En mí por ti me moría,
Y por ti resucitaba,
Que la memoria de ti
Daba vida y la quitaba.

XVIII

*A Poem by the same author which paraphrases
the Psalm, 'Super flumina Babylonis'*

Over the streams of running water
Which by Babylon are crowned,
There I sat, with bitter teardrops
Watering the alien ground.

I was full of your remembrance,
Sion, whom I loved of yore,
And the sweeter your remembrance
Bitterly I wept the more.

I cast off my costly garments,
Donned the working clothes you see,
And the harp that was my music
Hung upon a willow tree.

There to wait for the fulfilment
Of the hope I hoped in you.
There did love so sorely wound me
And my heart from me withdrew.

I intreated him to kill me
Since he'd wounded me so sore.
And I leaped into his fire
Knowing it would burn the more.

Now the fledgling bird excusing
Who would perish in the fire,
In myself I may be dying,
Yet from you my life respire.

In myself for you I perished
Yet through you revive once more,
Whose remembrance gives me life
Which it took from me before.

[79]

Gozábanse los extraños
Entre quien cautivo estaba.
Preguntábanme cantares
De lo que en Sión cantaba;
Canta de Sión un himno,
Veamos cómo sonaba.

Decid: ¿Cómo en tierra ajena,
Donde por Sión lloraba,
Cantaré yo la alegría
Que en Sión se me quedaba?
Echaríala en olvido
Si en la ajena me gozaba.

Con mi paladar se junte
La lengua con que hablaba,
Si de ti yo me olvidare,
En la tierra do moraba.

Sión, por los verdes ramos
Que Babilonia me daba,
De mí se olvide mi diestra,
Que es lo que en ti más amaba,

Si de ti no me acordare,
En lo que más me gozaba,
Y si yo tuviere fiesta,
Y sin ti la festejaba.

¡Oh hija de Babilonia,
Mísera y desventurada!
Bienaventurado era
Aquel en quien confiaba,
Que te ha de dar el castigo
Que de tu mano llevaba.

Y juntará sus pequeños,
Y a mí, porque en ti lloraba,
A la piedra que era Cristo,
Por el cual yo te dejaba.

When the aliens were carousing
Where a captive I was found,
They would ask me for a ditty
From my Country's distant bound:
'Sing for us a hymn of Sion,
Let us hear how well they sound.'

How can I sing here in exile
Where I weep against my choice
For my Sion, and the raptures
Which in Sion thrilled my voice.
I would hurl her to oblivion
If abroad I could rejoice.

May it join unto my palate—
This same tongue with which I speak,
If to slight my native country
I should ever prove so weak!

Sion, by the deep green branches
Which in Babylon I see,
May my own right hand forget me
Which I loved the most when free,

If I let slip from my remembrance
What I most enjoyed in you,
Or I celebrate one feast-day
Save it be within your view.

Daughter of the Babylonians
Luckless and unhappy maid!
Bless'd and happy was the Person
Upon whom my trust was laid,
By whom the weary chastisement
Of your own hand will be repaid.

He will join me with his children,
Because to you my tears were due,
And bring me to the Rock of Jesus
By which I have escaped from you.

XIX

Glosa a lo divino

Sin arrimo y con arrimo,
Sin luz y a oscuras viviendo,
Todo me voy consumiendo.

Mi alma está desasida
De toda cosa criada,
Y sobre sí levantada,
Y en una sabrosa vida,
Sólo en su Dios arrimada.
Por eso ya se dirá
La cosa que más estimo,
Que mi alma se ve ya
Sin arrimo y con arrimo.

Y aunque tinieblas padezco
En esta vida mortal,
No es tan crecido mi mal;
Porque, si de luz carezco,
Tengo vida celestial;
Porque el amor de tal vida,
Cuando más ciego va siendo,
Que tiene al alma rendida,
Sin luz y a oscuras viviendo.

Hace tal obra el amor,
Después que le conocí,
Que, si hay bien o mal en mí,
Todo lo hace de un sabor,
Y al alma transforma en sí;
Y así, en su llama sabrosa,
La cual en mí estoy sintiendo,
Apriesa, sin quedar cosa,
Todo me voy consumiendo.

XIX

With a divine intention

Without support, yet well supported,
Though in pitch-darkness, with no ray,
Entirely I am burned away.

My spirit is so freed from every
Created thing, that through the skies,
Above herself, she's lifted, flies,
And as in a most fragrant reverie,
Only on God her weight applies.
The thing which most my faith esteems
For this one fact will be reported—
Because my soul above me streams
Without support, yet well-supported.

What though I languish in the shades
As through my mortal life I go,
Not over-heavy is my woe
Since if no glow my gloom invades,
With a celestial life I glow.
The love of such a life, I say,
The more benightedly it darkens,
Turns more to that to which it hearkens,
Though in pitch-darkness, with no ray.

Since I knew Love, I have been taught
He can perform most wondrous labours.
Though good and bad in me are neighbours
He turns their difference to naught
Then both into Himself, so sweetly,
And with a flame so fine and fragrant
Which now I feel in me completely
Reduce my being, till no vagrant
Vestige of my own self can stay.
And wholly I am burned away.

XX

Glosa a lo divino del mismo autor

Por toda la hermosura
Nunca yo me perderé,
Si no por un no sé qué
Que se alcanza por ventura.

Sabor de bien que es finito,
Lo más que puede llegar,
Es cansar el apetito
Y estragar el paladar;
Y así, por toda dulzura
Nunca yo me perderé,
Sino por un no sé qué
Que se halla por ventura.

El corazón generoso
Nunca cura de parar
Donde se puede pasar,
Sino en más dificultoso;
Nada le causa hartura,
Y sube tanto su fe,
Que gusta de un no sé qué
Que se halla por ventura.

El que de amor adolece,
Del divino ser tocado,
Tiene el gusto tan trocado,
Que a los gustos desfallece;
Como el que con calentura
Fastidia el manjar que ve,
Y apetece un no sé qué
Que se halla por ventura.

XX

With a divine intention, by the same author

For all the beauty life has got
I'll never throw myself away
Save for one thing I know not what
Which lucky chance may bring my way.

The savour of all finite joy
In the long run amounts to this—
To tire the appetite of bliss
And the fine palate to destroy.
So for life's sweetness, all the lot,
I'll never throw myself away
But for a thing, I know not what,
Which lucky chance may bring my way.

The generous heart upon its quest
Will never falter, nor go slow,
But pushes on, and scorns to rest,
Wherever it's most hard to go.
It runs ahead and wearies not
But upward hurls its fierce advance
For it enjoys I know not what
That is achieved by lucky chance.

He that is growing to full growth
In the desire of God profound,
Will find his tastes so changed around
That of mere pleasures he is loth,
Like one who, with the fever hot,
At food will only look askance
But craves for that, he knows not what,
Which may be brought by lucky chance.

[85]

No os maravilléis de aquesto,
Que el gusto se quede tal,
Porque es la causa del mal
Ajena de todo el resto;
Y así, toda criatura
Enajenada se ve,
Y gusta de un no sé qué
Que se halla por ventura.

Que estando la voluntad
De Divinidad tocada,
No puede quedar pagada
Sino con Divinidad;
Mas, por ser tal su hermosura,
Que sólo se ve por fe,
Gústala en un no sé qué
Que se halla por ventura.

Pues de tal enamorado,
Decidme si habréis dolor,
Pues que no tiene sabor
Entre todo lo criado;
Sólo, sin forma y figura,
Sin hallar arrimo y pie,
Gustando allá un no sé qué
Que se halla por ventura.

No penséis que el interior,
Que es de mucha más valía,
Halla gozo y alegría
En lo que acá da sabor;
Mas sobre toda hermosura,
Y lo que es y será y fué,
Gusta de allá un no sé qué
Que se halla por ventura.

Do not amaze yourself at this
That pleasure is of earthly things
That cause from which most evil springs
And most the enemy of bliss.
And so all creatures earth-begot
Begin from it to turn their glance
And seek a thing, I know not what,
Which may be won by lucky chance.

For once the will has felt the hand
Of the Divine upon it set,
It never ceases to demand,
Divinity must pay the debt.
But since its loveliness to scan
Only true faith may steal a glance,
It finds it out as best it can
By risking on a lucky chance.

With love of One so high elated,
Tell me, if you would find great harm
If the servants He created
Did not rival Him in charm?
Alone, without face, form, or features,
Foothold, or prop, you would advance
To love that thing, beyond all creatures,
Which may be won by happy chance.

Think not that the interior sprite
Which is of vastly greater worth,
Can find among the joys of earth
Much for amusement or delight.
This world no beauty can advance
Which is, or ever was begot,
To vie with that, I know not what,
Which may be won by lucky chance.

Más emplea su cuidado
Quien se quiere aventajar,
En lo que está por ganar,
Que en lo que tiene ganado;
Y así, para más altura
Yo siempre me inclinaré
Sobre todo a un no sé qué
Que se halla por ventura.

Por lo que por el sentido
Puede acá comprehenderse,
Y todo lo que entenderse,
Aunque sea muy subido,
Ni por gracia y hermosura
Yo nunca me perderé,
Sino por un no sé qué
Que se halla por ventura.

XXI

Del Verbo divino

Del Verbo divino
La Virgen preñada
Viene de camino
Si le dais posada.

The man who strains for wealth and rank
Employs more care, and wastes more health
For riches that elude his stealth
Than those he's hoarded in the bank;
But I my fortune to advance
The lowlier stoop my lowly lot
Over some thing, I know not what,
Which may be found by lucky chance.

For that which by the sense down here
Is comprehended as our good,
And all that can be understood
Although it soars sublime and sheer;
For all that beauty can enhance—
I'll never lose my happy lot:
Only for that, I know not what,
Which can be won by lucky chance.

XXI

Concerning the Divine Word

With the divinest Word, the Virgin
Made pregnant, down the road
Comes walking, if you'll grant her
A room in your abode.

XXII

Suma de la perfección

Olvido de lo criado,
Memoria del Criador,
Atención a lo interior
Y estarse amando al Amado.

XXII

Summary of perfection

Ignoring the created and inferior;
Remembering above all things the Creator;
Attention to the life that is interior;
For the Beloved love that's always greater.